Preface

I am sure that, a few years from now, the period we are currently going through will be a subject for analysis and study in academic economic textbooks.

We are experiencing an unprecedented, complex, economic, financial, institutional and systemic crisis.

We have heard and read a great number of analyses and attempts at interpretation of the crisis but on an exclusively macroeconomic level and, in most instances, the explanations tend to be vague and inadequate.

When the negative impact of such a crisis becomes dramatic and reaches a lower level, practical solutions are required by every manager, businessman, investor, official, employee and householder.

This is what Michael Virardi provides in his new book. It is a valuable publication because it is to the point, practical and inventive.

Once again, Michael has surpassed himself and once again he has made his friends proud.

Makis Keravnos

CEO, Hellenic Bank Ltd
Former Minister of Labour & Social Insurance
Former Minister of Finance

To contact the author:

Address: 67, Agias Zonis St., 3090 Limassol, P.O. Box 50459, Cyprus
Tel: (+357) 99612532
Fax: (+357) 25375118
e-mail: michael@virardi.com

Translated from Greek by

John Vickers

Illustrations

Igor Varchenkom
(Nominated for "Best Cartoonist in the World 2011")

Design and Layout

Indigo Zone Ltd

Printed by

eSelis Print Center

ISBN 978-9963-2808-1-0

www.michaelvirardi.com

Michael R. Virardi

Crisis?
Let's
Beat it!

24
**Simple Ideas to
Boost Your Business
and Your Life**

For Christine,

my other half.

Without her,

nothing would be complete,

not even this book!

CYPRUS AUTISM
ASSOCIATION

10% of the proceeds from sales of this book will
be donated to support the excellent work of the Pancyprian
Association for Individuals with Autism

CONTENTS

INTRODUCTION

"You Need to be Croesus in a Crisis"

Aristotle Onassis

"Setting the bar higher" was the slogan at the Eureka company's Annual General Meeting which I had the good fortune to attend. Shortly before the end of the meeting, the Cypriot Paralympic Gold Medallist swimmer Karolina Pelendritou made her appearance. She was the guest of honour and keynote speaker. Her address may have lasted for about ten minutes but it stayed in my mind the whole evening.

Among other things, she referred to the fact that, like many ambitious champions, she is also one of those people who has difficulty waking up in the morning for her daily training, and that the glare of publicity lasts much less than the hours of persistent, solitary work away from the cameras. Karolina revealed that she always associates the sound of the Cyprus national anthem with the crowning glory of her efforts, as it played on two occasions: once in Beijing and once in Athens.

From everything that she shared with us, what made the greatest impression on me was her reference to the 'pain barrier', the point at which most athletes – and less often champion athletes – lose their strength and their will to keep trying. It is the point at which most give up the fight.

If an athlete, with the help of his/her coach and his/her own will and persistence, can manage to get through the pain barrier, new prospects open up and they lead to the achievement of goals.

It is the same stage that most Cypriot companies – and most companies around the world – have reached in recent years due to the financial crisis. It is the point at which companies, and perhaps the individuals that run them, feel that they have no future.

According to Karolina and the behaviour of champions, it is at this point that, first and foremost, we need to push ourselves towards new, better performances, passing through the pain barrier and, by making the extra effort, turning what looks impossible to most people into something feasible and real.

As a follow-up to my first book (Positive Impact! 26 Simple Ways to Boost Your Business and Your Life), the book you are holding aims to function as your 'coach' in every type of contest in which you are asked to take part in each aspect of your life. It comes to help you not only to get through the pain barrier but to expand your objectives by setting priorities, differentiating your actions, enriching your list of personal contacts, working on your personal development and behaviour and improving your performance by setting the bar even higher.

In this way you can consolidate your position by offering greater value to your clients/customers and associates. You can overcome the pain barrier and, like Archimedes, aptly shout "Eureka!" because your bar will already have been set very high.

On the following pages I present the experience of a large number of people who have either learnt from their continuous success or still learnt when they failed. Judgment – a person's ability to think deeply and reach the right conclusions – is presented in this book as a means of dealing with the financial crisis. But this judgment of yours, as a sensible person, requires constant 'movement' and functioning, it requires constant judgment. And how can you maintain your judgment in an unending crisis? By improving your performance, by finding smart and more productive techniques, by expanding your education through reading books. These are only some of the answers that you will find as you read on. Test yourself with this:

Count the number of times the letter 'F' appears in the following sentence:

> "FEATURE FILMS ARE THE RESULT
>
> OF YEARS OF SCIENTIFIC STUDY
>
> COMBINED WITH THE
>
> EXPERIENCE OF YEARS"

How many did you count? Did you find 4, 5 or all of them? (6 in total!) These days no 'F' can go missing, no detail can be overlooked. Mistakes must be kept to a minimum and efforts to a maximum. Because while everyone may consider the present time to be a "time of challenges", according to the Chinese it is also "an extremely interesting time".

The 24 simple ideas presented in this book will help you:

* **To excel, starting first and foremost by getting through the pain barrier.**

* **To make yourself stand out on both a professional and a personal level.**

* **To increase the likelihood of getting your day off to a positive start.**

* **To multiply your chances of keeping your job or finding one.**

* **To gain all the qualities that mark out a leader and a genuine individual.**

* **To set out and number your priorities.**

* **To achieve personal and professional development and success.**

At Princeton University, which I have been fortunate to visit, the celebrated scientist Albert Einstein once gave his students the same exam paper two years running. One of the students asked him why he had chosen to set identical questions for both years. His reply was immediate: *"This year all the answers are different!"* The same applies today. The questions/challenges may be the same but the answers/solutions in the modern financial and socio-political environment are different.

My own experiences, from the seminars and lectures that I have given to a plethora of individuals and organisations and from the successful implementation of the ideas and solutions that I have offered my attendees, have led me to write the book you are holding. It contains my own simple life stories that can become yours. The suggested ideas and solutions that have helped many successful people can become a tangible part of your life too.

As you go through the following pages, I hope that you will come to realise that the only stable thing is change. It is through change that your true value and worth will be revealed and it will help you stand out both professionally and personally.

Have a good journey through the pages of this book!

Michael R. Virardi

I

BEHAVIOUR - ATTITUDE

"Attitude is a little thing that makes a big difference."

Winston Churchill

You can be sure that, when faced with two or more candidates for a specific job, with identical qualifications, especially academic ones, companies today prefer to recruit a positive and optimistic individual rather than a negative and pessimistic one. The same applies to entrepreneurs who offer identical products or services: in the end, the preferred one will be more positive and optimistic than the rest.

The reason is simple. The optimistic person sees the positive side of things and situations, sees solutions where the negative person sees problems. He/she sees light at the end of the tunnel, by contrast with the negative one who sees 'darkness' everywhere.

Today, more than ever, displaying a positive attitude and behaviour is in itself a way of making yourself stand out and an additional qualification.

I am sure you know that no-one has ever erected a statue in memory of the most negative person in the world. A positive attitude is the key to dealing with even the most difficult of everyday situations. These days, being positive in your attitude and behaviour is an important component and a basic prerequisite not only for success but for survival.

By adopting an optimistic and positive attitude in a difficult situation, you give yourself a greater probability of dealing with and resolving a 'problem' more easily and quickly. At the same time, you gain an attitude that is free of the worry and stress that are the scourge of our times, thereby increasing your chances of becoming a happier and more successful person.

A positive attitude starts with positive thinking and behaviour; it is based on positive expectations, preparation and action and it ends with a positive assessment. When we talk about positive behaviour, we also mean integrity, taking the initiative, determination, self-criticism and leadership qualities. These are characteristics that should 'accompany' not only the young person of today but the experienced professional of tomorrow. So, in order to bring about positive results, you should also try to view the glass as half-full and not half-empty. Or if you want to be more positive than everyone else, you should view the glass as half-full of water and half-full of oxygen! The attitude you adopt depends on you. Choose a positive one!

By reading the articles in this section, you will:

- Understand the importance of integrity and sincerity.

- Realise how important it is to lead by example.

- Comprehend the significance of your choice to feel and act like a self-employed person.

- Appreciate the value of determination in your actions.

- Recognise the power of positive thinking.

1

A Painting Worth
a Thousand Words

One day my 11-year old niece Georgia Virardi came running
up to me, eager to show me one of her many paintings with
particular pride. Using all her artistic flair and a simple brush
and a few paints, she had chosen to depict a mountain and three
men. The first, who was the oldest and seemingly the wisest,
was sitting on the mountain top while the two younger ones,
right and left, were carrying their bags and attempting to climb
the mountain, heading in opposite directions. The two young
men would at some point meet with the wise old man on the
mountain's peak. I immediately asked Georgia to give me her
own explanation of what the painting was about. Naturally, the
little girl's painting brought to my mind the old saying, "A picture
is worth a thousand words".

The story is told about a young man who left his village, carrying all his worldly goods, to go and settle in the neighbouring village. When he reached the top of the mountain he met an old man and he asked him if he knew what the people were like in the village in which he was planning to settle down. Before the old man answered, he asked for the young man's own opinion of the people in the village that he was leaving. The young man, clearly disappointed and angry, told the old man that the people in his village were wretched, of bad character and dreadful behaviour, which was why he had taken the big decision to leave even his parents behind and to go and live in the next village. The old man then told him that the people in the village in which he intended to settle down had the same bad character and behaviour. The young man thanked the old man and continued on his way to his new life. The second young man who had similarly left his village – the one in which the first young man intended to live – in order to go and live in the first one's village also met the old man. When the old man asked him about the people of the village he was leaving, the young man could not have been more positive. He said that they were kind, just, polite, of excellent character and behaviour. The wise old man then used exactly the same words to describe the people of the village in which the second young man was planning to live.

This story shows that "you are not what you think you are but you are what you think".

In other words, if you are constantly thinking in a negative way and negative thoughts rule your mind, your results are likely to be negative too. If you think positively and fill your mind with positive thoughts, then the chances of achieving your goals and having a successful personal and professional life will increase considerably.

Moreover, research led by Karina Davidson of the Columbia University Medical Centre in the USA, which looked into the relationship between emotional states and the health of the hearts of 1,700 people over a period of 10 years, found that the so-called 'positive emotions' (joy, happiness, satisfaction, enthusiasm) reduced the risk of heart attack, angina or stroke by 22%. On the contrary, negative emotions (melancholy, grief, stress, worry, etc.) increase the risk of heart disease.

Similarly, a study by the University of Pennsylvania showed that optimistic individuals are more successful in business, education, sport and politics than their equally talented but pessimistic counterparts. On the basis of its own research, a well-known international Insurance Company developed a test so as to distinguish optimists from pessimists during the recruitment process. The results of this innovative approach were astonishing. The optimists who were taken on recorded 20% higher sales than the pessimists during their first year, while in the second year the difference soared to 50%. Over the past 25 years, more than 300,000 successful salespeople on high incomes have been interviewed by scientists trying to identify what they think about most of the time. Do you know what the thoughts of the highly-paid salespeople are? They are asking themselves what they want and how they can get it, how they can make it real. In contrast with those frightened salespeople who are constantly thinking about what they don't want to happen to them.

In the world of business but in life more generally, you are what you think. If you want to change the 'results' in your life, then you should start by changing your thoughts from negative to positive, and from positive to even more positive!

2

Self-employed or Not?

I recently had the opportunity and the honour to be a speaker at a General Insurance of Cyprus personnel meeting. The Chairman of the Board, George M. Georgiades, was the final speaker but he left his mark, engaging my interest and, at the same time, impressing his 110 associates who were present.

Mr Georgiades' reference to the present financial crisis revealed the need to give precedence to the values and ideals that we all espouse, irrespective of position or education. What became clear was the importance of being authentic, sincere, simple, immediate and accessible since we are serving arguably the best-educated and informed clients/customers of all time in an extremely competitive environment.

If we are to increase our chances of success with the above goal, Mr Georgiades noted the need to consider ourselves "self-employed" and to act as such; to work in such a way as to feel that the business belongs to us and that the success of our actions will guarantee the success of both our company and our own professional life. To achieve this, according to Mr Georgiades, we need to take on and display the characteristics of the self-employed individual in every aspect of our professional life.

Such characteristics and behaviour include responsibility, industriousness, optimism, a keen sense of urgency, inspiring trust, and the ability to persuade one's colleagues and to create new opportunities. The biggest mistake for a professional is to believe that he is working for anyone else but himself. If you really believe yourself to be "self-employed", all your positive philosophy and professional mentality will be visible not only to your friends and associates but to your internal and external clients/customers too.

I was impressed and particularly pleased by what I heard that night, especially from someone in such a high position in an important organisation. In my opinion, the difference between someone who acts as if "self-employed" and someone who neither feels nor acts like a "self-employed" person may be small but it is this small difference that brings about a major change. By acting as if "self-employed", you are making a conscious choice to implement the characteristics mentioned by Mr Georgiades in his address and you become part of the positive results and success of your organisation. On the other hand, their haphazard implementation or your decision not to

integrate these characteristics into your professional life is a way of behaving that you must be prepared to account for and to justify any failures of the company or of your own.

To feel that you are part of the success – or during the bad times, the failure – of your company, even if you are not an actual shareholder, not only helps you improve your performance in terms of responsibility, industriousness, optimism, a keen sense of urgency, inspiring trust and the ability to persuade colleagues and create new opportunities, but it helps you mainly to "shine" by gaining friends, associates, clients/customers and respect... As Odysseas Elytis said in his collection of essays entitled *The Garden of Illusions*,

"Man is but a flash of light; And if you saw, you saw"

So it is that we are all but a flash of light in this short life of ours and if we manage to shine in such a way as to be responsible for the positive memory that we leave behind us on a daily basis, then we shall have achieved something much more than merely improving our performance. We shall have left behind us a positive "legacy" in memories!

3

The Flat Tire

I recently read about a true story concerning the integrity of one's character and I would like to share it with you. It revolves around three students of Professor James Bonk who taught chemistry at Duke University in Durham, North Carolina, USA.

It was the end of the year and all that remained was the final examination. Three excellent chemistry students, full of self-confidence and sure of how they would perform, decided that, instead of revising on the last weekend before the exam, they would go and have a good time with some friends in Virginia.

After having so much fun and too much to drink, they realised that they would not be able to make it back to Duke in time for the Monday morning exam paper. So instead of sitting the exam, they made up a story to tell Professor Bonk. They told him that they had got a flat tire on their way back from Virginia, which had made it impossible for them to get back in time for the exam, and they asked the Professor to let them take the exam on Tuesday morning, instead of Monday with the other students.

After deliberating and, perhaps, thinking about the students' specific request, Professor Bonk decided to let them take the exam the following day. Relieved and delighted, the three students spent the whole of Monday night catching up on their revision. Believing themselves to be ready, they went to the exam centre on Tuesday morning. Professor Bonk put them in three separate rooms, gave each of them the exam paper, looked at his watch, told them how long they had and gave the signal for them to start writing.

The three of them opened the exam booklet and, with relief and pleasure, they saw that the first question, worth just 5 marks, was "What is the main component of air?" They each breathed a sigh of relief. "Perfect!" they thought. Such questions for a few marks and requiring brief answers were very easy for them and so they felt certain that they would do extremely well. Luckily the lie they had been obliged to tell would not cost them anything. Having answered the first question with relative ease, they turned the page to the second question…and the big shock. The second question, worth 95 marks was "Which tire?"

The story of the three students shows the importance of integrity to our character. Our behaviour, as expressed in our daily actions, reflects our integrity. Lies and efforts to fool clients/customers, associates or other people in various ways will, sooner or later, impose a personal and professional cost and lead to failure. Integrity means being what we say we are. The integrity of our words and actions is a basic element of success, in both our professional and personal lives. It is what brings us the respect and trust of others.

No "flat tire" can save the person who has lost his integrity.

PROBLEM WITH THE LEFT REAR TIRE!   PROBLEM WITH THE LEFT FRONT TIRE!

PROBLEM WITH THE RIGHT FRONT TIRE!

 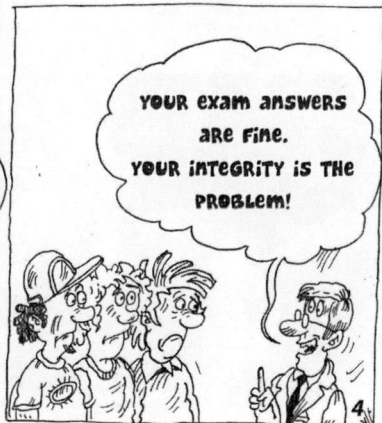

4

The Businessman
and the Mayor

During my very first visit to the office of a well-known businessman who owned a small-to-medium sized company in Limassol, one of the things that I noticed was that he didn't speak to any members of his staff as he walked along the corridor past their offices to his own.

This picture was enough to bring to mind the saying: "The way you treat your staff is exactly the same way that your staff will treat your customers!" And this thought proved to be correct a few minutes later when the businessman complained about how his staff dealt with customers while expressing his concern about the company's falling sales. This

was the reason why he had called me to his office and asked for my assistance.

We finished our first meeting and I left the company office, which is located very close to the Town Hall in Limassol. As I walked along, deep in thought about what guidance I could give the businessman to help not only himself but his staff and his customers, I witnessed what I would call an unusual sight: the Mayor of the town stooping – almost kneeling – to pick up litter on his way to his 'headquarters'!

On seeing this, I immediately looked around and admired my town. Limassol's rapid growth in recent years is due to a number of factors, the main one in my opinion being the strategy of realising a vision through teamwork. Of course, during any period of healthy development, there is always a leader who puts things on course by setting the right example through his/her behaviour and activity. By his action, the Mayor made me feel proud to be a citizen of Limassol and, at the same time, he charged me with the responsibility, as a willing, conscientious citizen, of ensuring that I play my part in keeping Limassol clean.

These two pictures of diametrically opposed ways of managing people, which I had seen in the space of a single day, reminded me of the quotation *"The best example of leadership is leadership by example"*. And this is how I worked out the guidance and advice that I would give the businessman. It would be good for our friend to consider that it is not enough to simply be positive, to show integrity, determination and consistency and to take initiatives. It is very important to lead by example and to ensure that, especially these days, our staff's behaviour shows excellence in the way they serve our lifeblood – our customers!

5

The 16-minute Difference

I read with great interest an article in the newspaper *Politis* entitled *"The 16-minute Difference"* about the massacre on 22 July 2011 of 69 young people on the Norwegian island of Utoya by Anders Behring Breivik. According to the newspaper, the mass murderer, who described himself as a "crusader defending Europe from the influx of Muslim immigrants" had earlier killed eight more people in a bomb attack in central Oslo.

The subtitle of the article was *"Police apologise for not arresting Breivik earlier!"* Speaking to reporters, the Norwegian Chief of Police, Oeystein Maeland, said among other things: "I apologize on behalf of the police that we were unsuccessful in capturing the gunman earlier. Every minute was one minute too long. It is a burden to know that lives could have been saved if the gunman had been arrested earlier".

The Norwegian Police report on its own reaction to the July 22 attacks revealed that the force was not adequately equipped to deal with attacks of such magnitude. Sissel Hammer, Chief of Police for the district responsible for Utoya, said that the police could "theoretically" have reached the island 16 minutes earlier. The calculation was based on the assumption that, if there had not been communication problems and a boat had been available (it was not), the police could have arrived on the island 16 minutes sooner. The telephone exchanges had become blocked which caused problems with the police's calls and their ability to form a clear and full picture of the situation, having received contradictory information about the existence of a large number of armed men on the island.

At the end of the day, by undertaking self-criticism, assessing your actions and, wherever necessary, as in this case, acknowledging your failings, you will stand out and you will be seen as a successful professional and a right-thinking person. Although we are not used to seeing leaders at all levels and ranks and in various areas of activity being self-critical, acknowledging their mistakes and offering a public apology, you can make a difference and be an innovator in this area. Don't be afraid to apologise. It will raise you in the eyes of your associates and employees. It will show your sincerity, your boldness and the deep sense of responsibility that characterizes you. It is one thing to make a mistake and another to admit it. Acknowledging one's failings and apologising are signs of resoluteness and a deep sense of security. They mark your start on a new, more successful course!

6

Change of Tack

What comes to mind when you hear the phrase "change of tack"? Think about it... Research has shown that for 80% of people hearing it, the connotations are the following: sea, rough sea, bad weather, captain, navy, storm, course, inconvenience, ship, waves, problems, lighthouse, wind. Personally, I think of something completely different. I think that it is never too late to do what we really want to and become what we truly wish to be.

Researchers in the United States studied 1,500 people over a 20-year period. They were divided into two groups, according to their choice of profession. Those in the first group, consisting of 1,245 or 83% of the total sample, had chosen their profession based on the prospect of immediate gain so as to be financially secure later on too. The second group, comprising the remaining 17% or 255 people, had chosen their profession on the basis of their interests, talents and wishes, in the knowledge that they might have concerns about their financial situation at a later stage. In other words, there was a possibility that they would not end up financially sound if they took up the career that they really wanted.

At the end of the 20-year research period, the results were unexpected. 101 of the 1,500 had succeeded in becoming millionaires. And with a single exception, they all belonged to the second group of those who had chosen to make a career of exercising the profession they loved. They were millionaires in a variety of ways. A millionaire is not only someone with a great deal of money. You can be a "millionaire" in terms of your health, a "millionaire" in the pleasure and satisfaction that you gain from the type of work that you have chosen to do, a "millionaire"

in experiences by enjoying unrepeatable, unique moments in your workplace and/or your personal or family environment. You can be a "millionaire" in relationships through your contacts with wonderful individuals who can only add value to your professional and personal life.

One of the greatest secrets of success, as I have discovered in more than 100 interviews carried out with successful businessmen for my third book on the subject of success, is "Love what you do and do what you love". This is precisely what Confucius wisely said: *"Choose the job you love and you will never need to work a day in your life".*

This should also be the main criterion in the choice of study by young people in these difficult times in which we are living. "Why shouldn't I choose a profession that will offer me financial security even if I don't like it?" is a question that any of today's young people might ask and the answer is very simple: because you will never excel at something you are forced to do which does not give you pleasure, you will never be one of the best in your field, you will never enjoy what you are doing and you will not like exercising your profession. If you do something that you love, irrespective of whether it is profitable, you have many possibilities of becoming a successful professional, one of the best in your field. This alone will bring you a great deal.

On the basis of which criterion did you choose what you do? It is never too late to do what you really want to and to become what you truly wish to be, if you have not already done so. It is never too late for a change of tack…

II

PERSONAL GROWTH

"Giving up is the ultimate tragedy"

Robert Donovan

Some 35 years ago, my father told me for the first time that "only your shares should be ordinary". At the tender age of five, I did not understand this piece of advice which, today, I consider very wise, given that I had no experience of life and had never owned company shares of any kind!

A few years ago I watched a very interesting television programme about the professional career of the evergreen Greek singer Yiannis Parios. During the programme, Parios referred to his father and, in particular, to the advice that he gave the singer at the start of his career: "Yiannis, take care to be better than ordinary. That's where things will start happening." Incredible but true!

For the past 40 years, Yiannis Parios has – in my opinion and that of thousands of his fans – remained at the very top of his profession by constantly reinventing and repositioning himself on the music scene and always being way above average.

It has been shown that most people choose to live within the bounds of the ordinary. They choose average, where little effort is required for improvement, where it is difficult to violate anyone's comfort zone and where so many friends, acquaintances and strangers not only choose to be on a daily basis but set the example for their children to follow.

Today, with 200 million people unemployed around the world and more than 50,000 registered unemployed in Cyprus (some of them good friends or even family members), with most Cypriot companies laying off staff rather than hiring and with the banks, the lifeblood of the economy, stating that loans are a luxury for the privileged few, living within the bounds of the average is extremely dangerous.

Would you seriously:

- Trust an "ordinary" doctor to carry out brain surgery?

- Be satisfied by an "ordinary" performance by your football team?

- Be happy if your customers describe your staff's service as "ordinary"?

If the answer to even one of these questions is "no", from now on you will want "ordinary" to describe your company's shares, not yourself!

By reading the articles in this section, you will:

❗ Realise that hearing is your greatest weapon.

❗ Recognise how and why it is important to get out of your comfort zone.

❗ Understand how important it is to improve even slightly on a daily basis.

❗ Comprehend why it takes 10,000 hours to become an excellent or first-rate professional.

❗ Learn to empty your glass of knowledge in order to allow it to fill up with new information.

7

Empty Your Cup

There was once an American University Professor who was close to completing a research paper on Zen philosophy. Shortly before publishing his research, and having written ten of its eleven chapters, he thought it proper to obtain the views of a Zen Master living in Japan. After a series of letters and telephone calls, he managed to arrange a meeting. He flew thousands of kilometres and then travelled hundreds more by train and bus in order to reach the wise man's village. He then had to walk uphill for two hours to the mountain top where he finally came across the Japanese Zen Master's hut.

As the Professor entered the humble hut, the wise old man welcomed him politely and asked what he could offer. The

Professor asked for some tea and the Zen Master began to fill a cup. At some point, the Professor noticed that the cup was overflowing with the tea that the Master was pouring and he began to shout: "Stop, stop! What are you doing? Can't you see that the cup is full?" The philosopher stopped, turned to the Professor and, with a disarming calmness, said: "I am doing exactly what you have been doing. You have come here with your cup of knowledge completely full. You have come with your own preconceived ideas and conclusions. You have come here with your study almost complete. What do you want from me? How can I explain the Zen philosophy and offer you new information when your cup is already full to the brim? When you have left no room for new knowledge and experiences?"

This is precisely what happens with most people. They work and go forward in their lives with their cup full to the brim. They filled it at some point in the past and they are convinced that they have learnt and done everything they had to learn and do. In this way they can relax and live with the illusion of success. Every day they come face to face with new challenges and new opportunities but, having the same way of thinking as they did yesterday, they let them pass by unexploited. They don't allow themselves to be exposed to new information, new solutions or even a simple book such as the one you are holding, which shows that you are not one of them.

However, the questions that arise are: What can we do? Where are we going with our full cup? How can we thrive and progress successfully with yesterday's knowledge and mentality in a world that is constantly changing? Albert Einstein is said to have

MEMORY...FULL!

LOADING...

given a partial answer to the question many years ago when defining insanity and explaining that "Insanity is doing the same thing over and over again but expecting different results."

So it's good to have a large bowl into which you can empty your cup, thus storing your knowledge so as to be able to use the cup at any time for new knowledge and ways of thinking. Empty your cup and let the new information that you will find in the coming pages of this book flow into it so as to help you enjoy a bright future!

8

The Killing Zone!

Cats and dogs are the most common pets in many parts of the world. In India, however, they have elephants instead! People keep elephants for company and, from an early age, they force them to remain confined by tying one of their legs by a rope to a wooden post in the garden. However much the young elephant may try to break free, it never manages to break the rope and get away.

Later, when the elephant has grown into a massive five-ton creature, something very strange happens. The same owners with the same rope and the same post continue to have the same – now enormous – elephant tied by the leg. And although this elephant now has enough strength to free itself in a second by breaking the rope, it never attempts to do so but remains tied up in the garden. Why is this? Because it learnt as a young animal that it can't free itself! The weakness and failure of childhood have become permanent and they will last for the whole of the elephant's life.

Today there are people who insist on behaving exactly like those pet elephants in India. They remain locked within their comfort zone since their efforts to go outside it failed in the past. In today's world of rapid developments in technology and unconfined competition, the one stable thing in our society is constant change. And you, too, need to be changing constantly in order to respond to the realities of the times and to develop what you are. You need to realise that, not only to survive but to excel, it is essential among other things:

- To provide excellent quality service to clients/customers which surpasses both their expectations and yours.

- To give value in every personal and professional transaction.

- To be clear in your mind that denial cannot help and to choose a positive way of thinking.

- To take initiative and to be responsible for your actions.

- To lead with integrity always.

- To have people as the reason for all your actions aimed at offering your company's products and services, always bearing in mind the words of Howard Behar, a former senior executive at Starbucks, who said, *"We're in the people business serving coffee, not the coffee business serving people"*. The same thing applies to us: we are not just running a company and serving people. Rather we are running a people-oriented company that happens to offer the services and products that we represent.

None of us was born with a life manual or a prescription for how our life will progress. No-one can impose conditions on our life. Yes, we may accept the advice of parents, teachers and friends but alone, making the most of our right to free choice, we choose our own course of action in this world. It is a course on which we aim to do the best we can but we frequently make mistakes. To make mistakes is not a bad thing; it is a learning opportunity, one that can help us become better people. It is a bad thing, however, to be so afraid of making mistakes that we keep to the well-travelled roads, to tried and tested behaviour and methods, thereby missing out on chances of doing something new and creative. Oscar Wilde, recognising the importance of erroneous behaviour, said: *"Experience is the name everyone gives to their mistakes"*.

Many people, feeling bored, remain trapped in their workplace and in their life in general because of their own choices. They have become victims of their comfort zones, they are afraid to make mistakes, afraid of failure and, therefore, they take no risks. People who consciously want to avoid the possibility of making a mistake are like those five-ton elephants that have remained roped to the posts of their early years. It is in your own hands to break the rope, free yourself from your comfort zone and make your dreams and ambitions come true by choosing your own course of action!

9

The Roots of our Habits

A wise teacher was walking through a dense forest with a young student. As they came close to a tiny plant, the teacher asked his student to uproot it. Within a fraction of a second and with no special effort, the student grasped it in the fingers of one hand and pulled it from the ground. "Now pull that one up," said the teacher, pointing to a sapling that was half a metre tall. With only the slightest difficulty the student uprooted the young tree. "Now try that one," the teacher told him, indicating a tree of the student's own height. By making a special effort, using all his body weight and the strength of his arms, the student succeeded in uprooting the tree, even though its stubborn roots put up some strong resistance. "Now," said the wise teacher," I'd like you to uproot that one…". Following his teacher's direction, the young man stared at an oak tree so tall that he could not see the very top. Aware of the superhuman effort he had put into uprooting the previous tree, he turned to his teacher and simply said, "I'm sorry, I can't".

"My son," he said to the young man, "you have just shown yourself the power of habit on you. The longer you have certain habits, the bigger they become, the deeper their roots go and the harder it is to pull them up. Some habits grow so big that you hesitate to even try and uproot them".

Studies carried out by psychologists have shown that 95% of what we feel, think, do and achieve is the result of learned habit. Of course, we are all born with instincts and without habits. We learn them (positive or destructive) in the course of time. Some of them, if not the majority, become as deeply rooted inside us as an oak tree in the ground and consequently it is extremely hard to "uproot" them. As leadership guru John C. Maxwell says, *"You will never change your life until you change something you do daily. The 'secret' of your success lies in your daily routine"*. It is no accident that what the great Greek philosopher Aristotle said thousands of years ago confirms Maxwell: *"We are what we repeatedly do"*. In other words, we are our habits. If we choose to live on automatic pilot, we are consciously allowing our habits to guide us.

In the book *Focal Point* by one of my mentors, Brian Tracy, the author explains how we can improve our life and our performance, meaning our habits, by 1000%! Yes, you read it correctly. Not 10%, not 20%, not 100% but 1000%! What Tracy proposes is that you improve yourself, your performance, your productivity and your income by one tenth of 1% each working day and rest at the weekend. This is equal to one thousandth.

We can all achieve what I call an infinitely small improvement and especially one thousandth. Do it every day of the week and you will have improved by 0.5% a week which is the equivalent of 2% a month and 26% a year. Your income will be doubling every 2.9 years. In the tenth year your performance and income should be around 1000% more than it is today. The advantage of Brian Tracy's proposal is that you do not need to make a 1000% greater effort or work 1000% harder today, which would not be humanly possible, but you simply improve by one tenth of 1% every day.

As my father Rolandos told me when I started work in the Virardi family business, to succeed I needed to realise that successful enterprises are like successful marathon runners. Those who win their races understand that that they need to maintain a steady performance throughout the race, a performance that has to be improved upon as time goes by. Exactly as Brian Tracy proposes in his book. You can make a start now on gradually improving yourself with small, steady steps each day.

10

Two Ears & One Mouth

God gave us two ears and one mouth and I think it would be wise to use them in the same proportion. *"We have two ears and one mouth so we may listen more and talk the less"*, as the Stoic philosopher Epictetus said some 2,000 years ago. It is obvious that someone who only talks will not learn anything new whereas someone who listens has a much greater chance of gaining new knowledge.

I was attending a seminar given by my friend Panicos Hadjiloizou when, for the first time, I saw the Chinese symbol for the verb "to listen": 原文. It is a multi-dimensional symbol which, as I discovered, contains the following six words:

TO LISTEN
=
YOU + EARS + EYES + HEART + UNDIVIDED ATTENTION

It sounds strange but it is absolutely true! A simple little word, a seemingly simple action such as "to listen" contains six more important words. It starts with "You", since you are the one who must listen if you wish to learn. And to do so means that you must give it your undivided attention, using your ears, eyes and heart. Listening with your heart means listening with emotion. It is this emotion that will make you a likeable listener, thereby gaining the appreciation and trust of your interlocutor.

The likeability and trust that you will gain make the selling of any product or service easier at all levels: from the 'sale' that a mother tries to close with her young daughter as she tries to persuade her to go to bed early, to the "selling" of himself that an out-of-work graduate attempts during an interview with the aim of persuading his would-be employers to give him a job.

By creating feelings of likeability and trust in your associates and customers, you are taking a step towards a successful "sale" every time. You are turning into action the saying that *"the heart is closer to the pocket book than the mind"*! In other words, people take decisions based on emotions and they justify them using their mind.

Although many people believe that listening is to be passive, it is, in fact, the opposite. Hearing is passive but listening means being completely active in a way that helps your professional and personal growth and prosperity. By listening actively and, moreover, by taking notes, you automatically gain the advantages of learning, of questioning what you already know and of building up new knowledge. There are three reasons why a salesperson (or indeed any person) should keep notes when coming into contact with a potential client/customer, associate or friend.

❗ When you keep notes, you won't forget.

❗ When you keep notes, you won't forget what the other person says and this action alone brings you closer to him/her in a magical way. It makes you more likeable as a person and, as a result, your chances of cooperation increase. Your interlocutor feels "important" because what he/she has to say is clearly so important that you "take the trouble" to write it down. In this way you are showing your appreciation of the other person and what he/she says.

❗ When you keep notes you have a better chance of remembering "to close the sale with the same words that your customer used when he answered the question about his greatest need". This is perhaps the most important reason for keeping notes, especially when closing a sale.

The following example from my own experience explains the above in the best way. When I was training salespeople at Unicars (representatives of Audi, Volkswagen, Skoda and Seat vehicles in Cyprus), I referred to the three reasons why we should keep notes. Regarding the third reason, I used the example of a customer who enters the showroom and the first thing he tells us that he wants a car with good road holding so

1.

2.

as to drive every day from Paphos to Nicosia and back without tiring himself and, in particular, without straining his waist which has been giving him trouble for years. According to the third reason why we should keep notes ("to close the sale with the same words that your customer used when he answered the question about his greatest need"), the salesperson should refer to all the positive aspects and advantages of the particular model and end by noting that the greatest advantage is the fact that the car has fantastic road holding qualities. This alone differentiates this salesperson from any other by showing that he is a good listener, thereby increasing his chances of closing a deal with the customer.

On thinking about all this, I would say that it is not at all by chance that the 18th century French novelist Honoré de Balzac once wrote, *"If you talk all the time, you will always be right"*! Do you want to be always right? Don't rush to answer. Listen well…use your heart…keep your notes…and then give your answer!

11

"Mum, you don't listen to me!"

The meeting I had with my good friend Diana turned out to be very constructive, since she confided in me and told me her personal story, a story starring herself and her young son Eli who taught her to give people her undivided attention when listening to them.

It all began one day when Eli arrived home very excited and clutching an invitation to the birthday party of his best friend Makis. He gave his mother the invitation and every day he would remind her about the day of the party. Diana promised her impatient son that by Makis' birthday she would be ready with a present.

After 29 reminders, the big day finally arrived. It was a Saturday and, sitting in a chair at the hairdresser's, Diana was sure that she had everything under control. Her thoughts were interrupted by a phone call from Eli. She answered abruptly and hung up even more abruptly after threatening her son that if he called her again he wouldn't go to the party. At the other end of the line, all Eli managed to say was "Mum…" and the phone went dead.

At 3.00pm, Diana and her sister arrived home to pick up Eli and take him to the party. Clearly annoyed, Eli sat silently in the back of the car as Diana and her sister studied the invitation to work out how to get to Makis' house. To their surprise, they saw that the party was not starting but finishing at 3.00pm! With one foot inside the car and the other outside, a bitter Eli turned to Diana and said, "Mum you don't listen to me, you never listen to me… that's your problem! If you'd listened to me even a bit you'd have known that the party started at 12 and finished at 3!"

The good part of the story is that after this event, which really upset her, my friend Diana put into practice the saying "When you lose, don't lose the lesson" and today she is possibly one of the best listeners I have ever met. She realised clearly that God gave us two ears and one mouth and that it would be wise, if we wish to reduce our mistakes, to use them in the same proportion!

All those around you have something to teach you; you can learn from them. Just stop for a moment and listen to them. Even if you hear things you disagree with, you can use them in your own way in the course of your life. Learn to listen calmly and patiently with all your mind and heart. Be focused on the person talking to you and show the necessary respect. His/her words may conceal big or small secrets to make your personal life better and your professional career more successful. Are you listening?

12

10,000 Hours

In 2002 I had the good fortune to attend a seminar in Charlotte, North Carolina by Jeffrey Gitomer, arguably the best sales consultant in the world. Once the day-long seminar was over I approached him to ask him about something that had been spinning in my mind from the start: what did I need to do in order to become as successful as him in the same profession? I shall never forget his answer for two reasons: because he really did tell me the "secret of success" and because I was surprised as soon as I heard what he had to say. He told me that in order to become so successful I needed to study the subject I chose to specialise in for 2-3 hours every day, taking a break at weekends, and when I had done that, to contact him again in ten years' time!

Just recently, and shortly before contacting Gitomer to inform him of my progress – I had done what he told me and the 10-year period was almost up – I read *Outliers*, a very interesting book by the bestselling author Malcolm Gladwell. In the book, the African American writer claims that you need 10 years or, put differently, 10,000 hours, to gain true expertise in your field.

Using examples from true events in the life of The Beatles, he notes that even such a successful group did not become so overnight. The Beatles were playing music for no less than 7 hours every night for 7 years in various unknown bars in Hamburg in what was then West Germany. It is calculated that they played more than 1,200 gigs prior to 1964, gradually building their career until they gained success and became the idols that they still are today.

According to the neurologist Daniel Levitin, who has carefully studied the formula for success, 10,000 hours are required for the brain of an individual to assimilate everything it needs to know to reach the stage of true expertise in a given field. This applies, Levitin says, to lyric writers, basketball players, pianists, chess players, writers, and even criminals! According to Levitin and his team of researchers, not one person has been found so far to have become an expert in his field with less than 10,000 hours or 10 years' study.

Looking back on my own experiences, I have come to the conclusion that both Gitomer and Levitin are absolutely right. The proof of this can be seen in my professional career. I studied for 7-8 consecutive years and I didn't have a single client for my seminars. Or rather I had not managed at that point to persuade anyone to believe in me and trust me. I listened to Gitomer, turned his words into action and, at the same time, I was patient until an opportunity came along and I seized it, always keeping in mind the saying "Luck is where preparation meets opportunity".

Today I am in the happy position of holding dozens of seminars and lectures every year and I have succeeded in multiplying both my knowledge and my income. How did I do it? By using my two ears and one mouth and investing more than 8,000 hours to date in studying my subject and recognising that the "secret of success" is nothing more than the investment in hours of continuous study of the subject you love. You just need to discover what it is that you love and… don't worry. I promise you that one day, sooner or later, you will find it, just as I did at the age of 29!

III

SETTING PRIORITIES

"There is never enough time to do everything,
but there is always enough time
to do the most important thing".

Brian Tracy

It was Denis Waitley who said, *"Time is an equal opportunity employer. Each human being has exactly the same number of hours and minutes every day. Rich people can't buy more hours.Scientists can't invent new minutes. And you can't save time to spend it on another day. Even so, time is amazingly fair and forgiving. No matter how much time you've wasted in the past, you still have an entire tomorrow."*

Success is guaranteed when you make the best possible use of your time, by having a schedule and setting priorities. Time is worth more than money because you may be able to find more money but you won't find more than 24 hours in a day. Not making the most of your time is like not making the most of the opportunities given to you to succeed!

As I said on my CD entitled *11 open secrets to help you increase your sales,* in the final analysis your whole life up to now – i.e. your way of life, your car, your house, your bank account, etc. – is the result of how you chose to make use of and "exchange" your time in the past. Put simply, you are your time! And your choices on matters of making the most of your time have led to your results today, making up the "picture of your life".

If, as a professional, you find it hard to combine increased responsibilities, family obligations and too little time, you are not the only one. The importance of proper time management can be seen in the results of a survey in which, to the question "What is your greatest challenge at work?", some 46% of 1,400 polled Financial Controllers replied "time management".

"If you want to make good use of your time, you've got to know what's most important and then give it all you've got" said the American manager Lee Iacocca. The ability to identify and prioritise the most important of a host of pending issues is an important leadership skill and a key element in the achievement of your goals. Try to use it while you read the following section.

By reading the articles in this section, you will:

- Realise the importance of setting priorities and goals in your life.

- Understand the importance of learning to prioritise and to make the most effective use of your time.

- Be inspired by the 80/20 rule.

- Choose to think on paper, i.e. to write down your thoughts.

13

The Dog and the Three Cats

My friend Marios Mavrides, an economist and currently (2013) a Member of Parliament in Cyprus, once asked me how important it is to set goals. I answered him using this example: a dog was chasing a cat until a second cat appeared on the road, at which point it stopped chasing the first one to run after the second. It did this until a third cat appeared and the dog abandoned its efforts, only to chase after the third cat this time. When, at the end of the day, the dog was asked how conscientious and hardworking it was, it replied, "Extremely. I didn't stop for a minute!" But when it was asked how productive a day it had been, the disappointed dog replied, "Not at all productive!" Its day was not productive because the dog did not have a clear goal. Instead, its goal changed each time and not by the dog itself but by whichever cat ran across his path.

THREE? NO! NOT even one!

So although we know that dogs can't talk (at least not our language) we understand that this story wants to tell us that "if you don't know where you are going, you won't go anywhere, no matter how hardworking and conscientious you are". Successful businesspeople think and talk constantly about what their goals are and how they can achieve them. The more often you think about your goals, the more focused on them you will be and the more positive and enthusiastic you will become, thus increasing the chances of surpassing not only your own limits but the limits of those who are not as focused on their goals as you are.

Studies have shown that salespeople who are focused on their goals are positive and enthusiastic, surpassing in sales 5-10, perhaps 20 times the average of their counterparts who are constantly thinking about their problems and their limitations. In the words of B.S. Walsh: *"If you don't know where you are going, how can you expect to get there?"*

In Lewis Carroll's classic children's book *Alice's Adventures in Wonderland*, there is a wonderful dialogue with a deep message about setting goals:

> *"Would you tell me, please, which way I ought to go from here?"*
>
> *"That depends a good deal on where you want to get to,"* said the Cat.
>
> *"I don't much care where –"* said Alice.
>
> *"Then it doesn't matter which way you go,"* said the Cat.

Professionals in their field and the Cat in the story know something that Alice in Wonderland and some inexperienced people and amateurs don't know. And that is nothing more than the saying, *"You can't hit a target you can't see, and you can't see a target you don't have"*. It would be wise, therefore, to prepare from the beginning of the year, knowing beforehand what the target is that you will fight to succeed in hitting. It would also be useful to do something that I have done for a number of years, something I took from my friend Darren Hardy, Editorial Director of *Success* magazine and author of the book *The Compound Effect*, in order to monitor the rate of my progress towards the achievement of my goals so as to make the necessary adjustments to them and to adopt similar behaviour and a similar way each time. In his book, Darren Hardy presents a guide to setting goals which he calls the Weekly Rhythm Register (you can download it from *http://michaelvirardi.com/weekly_register_en.pdf* in which you can see my goals and behaviours as an example for setting your own goals and adopting your own behaviours. To put it simply, this guide will help you to set your own goals and monitor the results to see your achievement rate. At the end of the day, your combined results will be tomorrow's indicator of your success!

It is wise and beneficial to your professional development and personal recognition if, first and foremost, you have goals and are focused on them. It is not by chance that the great American writer Zig Ziglar once said, *"Focus on your goals. People do not wander around and then find themselves at the top of Mount Everest"*. Think about it… What are your goals?

14

The Failure and Success of Preparation

While studying *The 21 Indispensable Qualities of a Leader*, the extremely interesting book by author and leadership guru John C. Maxwell, I was particularly impressed by the story of how lions are tamed. He mentions, among other things, how experienced animal trainers use a stool when they enter the lion's cage because it tames the lion better than any other object, apart from a rifle with tranquillizer bullets of course. As the lion tamer holds the stool with its four legs raised towards the animal, the lion tries to focus on all four legs at the same time. This paralyses and disorientates it. The animal's divided attention thus disorganises it and makes it blindly obey orders and become tamed.

Something similar happens in the case of people. Our fragmented attention disorientates us from our goals and distances us from success. We need to be effective in what we do and this depends on our ability:

1.   To set priorities in order of importance and
2.   To concentrate on our goal with all our focus and attention.

To achieve maximum effectiveness it is essential that we do both of the above. If you have priorities but no focus you will fail to complete almost anything you begin. And if you have focus but no priorities you will do what you do well but without the corresponding progress and development. As Brian Tracy said, *"There is never enough time to do everything, but there is always enough time to do the most important thing"*. This is why you need to set priorities.

I spent 18 months interviewing 101 successful businesspeople and, among the results of my research, was the emergence two characteristics that can be said to be typical of the successful entrepreneur. One was that 91% (92 of the 101 interviewees) work with a list which, in most cases, is written on an ordinary piece of paper. It is the same thing that a well-organised housewife has with her when she goes shopping. She takes the list with everything she needs to buy and, in this way, she not only gains time when searching for the products she wants but she increases her chances of not buying unnecessary items. The use of a list is, in the last analysis, a way of saving both time and money.

The second characteristic of the successful businessperson, in 90% (91 of the 101 interviewees), was that every day they prepare for the next day, every week for the following week and, at the start of each new year they set goals for the whole of the year. Proper preparation and timely planning of the next day, week and year can provide strong foundations for the successful achievement of our goals.

This is what I am in the habit of doing every Friday in order to prepare my schedule for the coming week. I take a piece of paper and divide it into five columns, one for each working day. I then divide each of these with two horizontal lines into three parts. The first represents my morning's work, the third is the afternoon and the second is for any business lunches that may arise. On Friday I fill in all my planned activities for the following week.

EVERYONE CHOOSES HIS/HER OWN WAY!

Through my own experience and my relations with businesspeople in Cyprus and abroad, I have learned that organised people are always prepared and thus they "oblige" their associates to follow their schedule since they know in advance what they will be doing each day. And this makes them effective.

These two characteristics should be firmly fixed in the mind of every professional, experienced or inexperienced, who wishes to secure a bright future by focusing his actions on specific areas and making the most effective use of his time. The secret of the success of your actions lies in your willingness to prepare because it goes without saying that if you fail to prepare you must automatically prepare to fail!

15

The 80/20 Rule

A few years ago I began work as a Business Consultant with a young businessman who expressed himself in a particular way that I totally opposed. His favourite phrase, which he would repeat every 15-20 minutes and feel its meaning intensely, was "I'm drowning!" According to the Law of Attraction and my friend Elenitsa Potamitou, a Law of Attraction Practitioner, the words and phrases that we use are like brushstrokes which, by themselves, mean nothing but once combined can create a masterpiece of art. In the same way, the words we speak can transform our present way of thinking and the picture of tomorrow's reality.

Anyone can understand why I am in favour of positive expressions and words, even when we want to show our concern about something that is bothering us. In this particular case, the young businessman was concerned about the fact that he never had enough time available to take care of his obligations and was incapable of managing this problem.

So I, in turn, made him aware of the 80/20 rule, otherwise known as the Pareto Principle. During our second meeting at his office, I had already told him that there is never enough time to do everything, but there is always enough time to do the most important things. This was shown by the Italian economist Vilfredo Pareto at the start of the 20th century who noticed that in Italy at the time, 80% of the population owned 20% of the wealth and that 20% of the population owned 80% of the wealth. In other words, the money was in the hands of the few. In the course of time, this rule was investigated by experts who concluded that it applies to almost everything we do in our daily lives but mainly in what has to do with our business.

The main message of this rule is that 80% of the results of something we do will come from 20% of our efforts. The rule can be applied in many instances in business and in our everyday life. Below are a few interesting examples. According to the 80/20 rule:

- 80% of our sales come from 20% of our products and services.

- 80% of our profit comes from 20% of our customers.

- 80% of our sales come from 20% of our salespeople.

- 80% of our results come from 20% of our actions.

- 80% of our production comes from 20% of our total working hours.

The young businessman understood right away that the time he consumed needed to fluctuate around 20% of his activities. In other words, his ability to focus on a few specific things, by applying the 80/20 rule, would bring success, whereas his inability to do this would bring stress, annoyance, failure and expressions like "I'm drowning".

When he decided to put the 80/20 theory into practice, the result, as he told me himself, was impressive. He faithfully implemented the Pareto Principle and soon noticed that, of his 82 customers, just 10 of them were responsible for 90% of his turnover. This shocking realization led him to take some simple and effective actions which, he said, completely changed his professional and personal life. A life which, until then, was totally consumed by his business, leaving no time for family and friends, no time for himself, putting his health at considerable risk due to the stress caused by his work.

He stopped contacting all his customers and pressurising them to order products. He noticed that his 10 biggest customers required special treatment and so he focused on them. These 10 most important customers ("Dream Customers" as we called them) would receive a package every month with a card thanking them for their cooperation and support. In the package there would be an easy-to-read book with useful advice on how to grow their business and how to help themselves and their associates develop. We increased the number of visits to these 10 customers from two to four times a month. The objective of these visits was to pay greater attention to the customers, to discover their future business needs, their habits and interests. We came so close to them that we increased turnover by 15%. It was logical that the 80% of our customers responsible for around 20% of our turnover (72 customers) would reduce their purchases from us and they did, but to our pleasant surprise not to the extent we expected. Turnover from the 80% of our customers fell by just 3% of the total, although productivity of the company and its employees rose. There was now more time to focus on the 20% of our customers – the 10 most important ones – but also, perhaps for the first time, time to set out a new course and strategy for the company. The young businessman began to contact important people who would probably bring additional value to the company with their ideas, knowledge and work.

Have you thought about how many of your customers are responsible for most of your profit? What are the products that guarantee you the most sales? Have you ever wondered where you are wasting time and money? Perhaps on things that are not very important or on customers who bring you much less than what you would expect?

Apply the 80/20 rule to your debtors and you will find what the young businessman and I, too, discovered in the Virardi family business. You will discover that 20% of them owe 80% of what is

owing to your company. In other words, if you have 100 debtors owing you €1,000,000, around 20 of them will owe €800,000 and the other 80 will be responsible for the remaining €200,000. It would therefore be wise to focus on the 20 who owe you the €800,000 since with fewer phone calls (around 20) and perhaps less effort you will receive more (€800,000) than if you focus on the 80 customers who owe you €200,000 and for which you will need to make a greater effort to collect less money (around 80 calls for €200,000).

The secret, so that you don't find yourself "drowning" like the young businessman before we met, lies first and foremost in your preparation. The best and most successful businesspeople in the world are prepared and organised in accordance with the Pareto Principle, otherwise known as the 80/20 rule.

16

The Fastest Train

I recently received an interesting e-mail about the most modern trains in the world. There is intense competition between China, Japan and the United States for which country has the most up-to-date train!

I presented this e-mail at one of my seminars on Self-Management and Time Management and I asked those present if they knew not only what the most modern train in the world was but also which one was the fastest.

After ten minutes and a storm of different opinions, which in some cases almost turned into a conflict, I gave them the answer: the fastest train in the world is the train of thought. Our thoughts can travel up to 289km per hour[1]. The journey can include so many things. How many of them can we maintain and keep alive? It is said that *"the most powerful memory is weaker than the faintest ink"*, meaning that if you want something to happen, you have a greater probability of it happening if you write it down. The reason is simple: the average person has 60,000 thoughts every day. How many of them can you store in your memory and then bring back?

The successful and organised person understands what leadership guru John C. Maxwell meant when he said "Every day you are either repairing or preparing". In other words, you are either preparing for tomorrow or "repairing"

---

[1] It was announced in December 2012 that China is working on a so-called 'bullet train' that will travel at 310mph but until it comes into operation my claims about the train of thought remain valid.

yesterday because you failed to prepare. So a notebook and a pen which are permanently in our pocket or bag become "weapons" with which we record our thoughts, making them real and accessible at any given moment. In his classic book *Think and Grow Rich*, the world-famous writer Napoleon Hill reminds us that *"Whatever the mind can conceive and believe, it can achieve"*.

Our train of thought, however, stops at many stations before reaching its destination. It may stop because "we failed" to record our idea on paper or because we let time pass and our memory fade. Perhaps, also, because others placed obstacles on our tracks, discouraging and preventing us from reaching our destination. Finally, perhaps we ourselves were afraid to set our train in motion.

I recently read this: *"A ship in a harbour is safe, but that is not what ships are built for"*. So don't let your thoughts and dreams fly away and be lost. Write them down and bring them to life. Dare to set the 'train' or 'ship' in motion because you never know where it might take you. And above all, always remember that life is so short that, in the end, it really is worth enjoying the journey!

IV

DIFFERENTIATION

"In real estate, it's location, location, location.
In business, it's differentiate, differentiate, differentiate."

Robert Goizueta

When the hourglass that measures our time in this world is almost empty, most people – and that includes you – would like to leave something behind. This "something" can only be offered, in my view, through differentiation.

You may be wondering why. For the simple reason that today's businesses, perhaps more than ever, are operating and growing in an extremely competitive environment. This tough competition exists on a personal level, too, due mainly to the high unemployment that we can see today on a global, European and local scale. A classic and recent example is that of a well-known company to which I provide consultancy services, which advertised a vacancy for a marketing assistant. 150 people applied for the job. For the same position in 2006, there were just 9 applications!

Differentiating material resources but mainly human resources is, perhaps, the only possible response to the constantly changing circumstances of the present reality of our market. The ability to differentiate immediately and successfully is an element of productivity and success. To manage to stand out as an individual or a company among people or organisations by offering excellent service, approaching the customer in a polite manner and maintaining bridges of communication with those around you is, of itself, not mere differentiation but certain success.

Differentiation helps you stand out from the crowd, attract attention, increase your chances of being selected for a job or continue in your present employment and it promises you a bright personal and professional future. If you are not pleased with your results and you continue to do what you have always done, you will continue to "receive" what you have always received up to now. If, however, you are not satisfied with this, then today is the time to start bringing differentiation into your personal and professional life!

By reading the articles in this section, you will be in a position to:

! * Discover ways in which you can be different and stand out from the crowd.

* Draw inspiration from the stories of people who have differentiated themselves from the rest.

* Understand the importance of being passionate about doing what you really love.

* Try and build bridges of communication with people, even when it appears that you are heading down different roads.

17

The Xenophon In You

It could be said that what distinguishes an ordinary person from an exceptional one is a fine line, something very small. On meeting Xenophon, however, you will realise at once that this is not the case. You will discover huge differences between an ordinary and an exceptional person and the reason is that Xenophon is a truly exceptional professional in his field.

I met Xenophon when he served me for the first time at the café I frequent. He welcomed me in a strong, firm voice, with eyes wide open and a gesture in my direction, implementing what I call today the "threefold welcome": "Hello, welcome, how can I help you?" and all this with a smile. I was startled! I didn't respond at once because I was so pleasantly surprised that I needed more than a couple of seconds to realise that I had just received excellent service, something which is generally considered to be something of a rarity by Cypriot standards.

After the first pleasant shock, I took my coffee and sat down in such a position as to purposely keep Xenophon in my sights and to discreetly observe his movements. The picture was equally disarming. His movements were full of energy, almost as if he was dancing, and he was clearly enjoying what he was doing. His permanent smile, combined with his good mood and the fact that he remembered and addressed all his customers by name, created a tremendous impression on me. Unprecedented service! Actions that would surprise even the American or European visitor who is used to such an exceptionally high standard.

In recognition of the fact that someone was offering superb service that was beyond any expectations and raising the bar even higher, I felt obliged to ask Xenophon his name. As a professional trainer, I have often been called upon to identify what goes wrong in customer service. In this case, however, which was perhaps one of the rarest in my career, I could see what was right and I was enjoying it!

Recently Xenophon surprised me yet again when, around 8pm, he telephoned me. In his characteristic Canadian Greek accent, he said, "Michael, good evening! I'm calling to say a big 'thank you' because I was told that you mentioned me in an interview on 94.8 FM about excellent customer service. Wow, man! Thanks a lot. That never happened to me before".

An exceptional individual can make a big difference, even in an average organisation, because he can affect others. Indeed, as time went by I noticed that the service provided by Xenophon's colleagues had improved considerably. Xenophon functioned as a role model for them. He may be a mere barman but he gives status and value to the work he does, believing that there is no such thing as an unimportant position or job but rather that there are people who feel unimportant because of what they do. Xenophon taught me that the job doesn't determine your performance but your performance will determine your job and, by extension, your income.

And because, as I have already mentioned, the word 'ordinary' should only apply to your company shares, anyone can follow Xenophon's example by choosing to be exceptional and to live an unusual and successful professional and personal life.

Your greatest advantage these days is your ability to exceed the expectations of your friends and clients/customers, to add value and pleasantly surprise those around you. The secret does not lie in advertising or investing thousands of euros but in imagination, creativity and in seeking the exceptional.

As I learned from Xenophon, providing good service is not an obligation but an opportunity. It is your opportunity to leave your positive mark on society, to show your worth, your chance to build bridges of communication, to meet and be recognised by established professionals and future friends. It is your opportunity to have your work recognised and praised by someone like me. It is your opportunity to choose to become an "exceptional Xenophon"!

18

Impeccable Service

I would never have imagined that a chance meeting for coffee would lead me to hear one of the most vivid and to-the-point true stories concerning impeccable customer service.

Not long ago I met up with Chris Yiallourides, a friend and one of my mentors. We sat down to have coffee and, as Chris was recalling his student days in the French city of Lyon, he remembered a significant event that had occurred while he was working for a well-known European supermarket chain. It was a chance but unprecedented occurrence, unusual but noteworthy and one that he felt worth sharing with me (and now, through me, with you).

Chris was working in one of the chain's branches and was responsible for stacking, properly presenting and maintaining the vegetables in the supermarket. Although it was a rainy winter day, the supermarket was packed with shoppers. At some point an elderly, serious-looking man approached Chris and asked him where he could find a specific brand of soap. Chris had two choices: to give the customer directions so that he could go and find the soap he wanted by himself, or to take him to the particular shelf and give him the product he was looking for. Without a second thought, he took the gentlemen to the personal hygiene section and handed him the soap. And before leaving, he offered to help the customer with anything else he might require. The elderly man, with evident satisfaction in his expression, replied politely that Chris had already done plenty for him.

Half an hour had not gone past when an announcement was heard over the supermarket's sound system. His poor French was enough for Chris to understand that he was being asked to go to the General Manager's office. His feelings of concern and bewilderment were intense. Why was he being called? What had happened? Was something bad in store for him? These thoughts were spinning around his mind during the five minutes it took him to reach the office. As he entered, he saw two men in front of him. Apart from the General Manager, he was surprised to see the elderly, grey-haired man whom he had served 30 minutes earlier.

The General Manager asked Chris at once if he knew the man standing next to him and Chris answered truthfully that the only thing he knew about him was the brand of soap he had asked for and which he had helped him find. Without further ado, the General Manager revealed that the elderly customer was in fact the majority shareholder in the company, a man respected by the whole of the firm's management and others!

Unable to utter a word, Chris received the sincere congratulations of the polite shareholder for his impeccable service, which stemmed from his positive stance and his immediate initiative to satisfy the customer. As if that was not reward enough, the highly esteemed gentleman offered Chris and his girlfriend (now his wife) Paola a dream trip to the Canary Islands, paid for by the company. And the culmination of all this – the real reward for his impeccable service – was that Chris was offered a management position in the company that he could take up once he had finished his studies. And all this because his first thought was the customer and how to serve him best!

Some might say that the difference between an ordinary and an extraordinary person is merely the prefix "extra-" in front of the word "ordinary" but there is much more to it than that. It is the same "extra" that we should all be trying to give to each of our contacts with clients/customers, associates, friends and family members. It is the "extra" that distinguishes us and our companies in a competitive environment. It is that small extra effort, such as the one that Chris made, that can bring about an "extra" reward. And although we shall probably never win a trip to the Canary Islands for our extra effort, we shall have gained something more permanent and long-lasting: the appreciation and respect of our clients/customers and our fellow-men!

19

Goodbye = Au Revoir

Until a few years ago, I knew very well that a full-page advertisement in a top-selling Cypriot newspaper was a major investment and was used almost exclusively to announce important and, usually, good news. We often see and read advertisements by a company or organisation for new and/ or existing products or services, as well as announcements concerning significant agreements with important clients, the purpose of which is to increase the value and respect of the company in question in the eyes of the public and, ultimately, to attract new clients. All of this in a full-page advertisement that we come across as we read the newspaper.

On 3 March 2010, however, page 9 of the newspaper *Phileleftheros* completely changed my view of full-page advertisements.

How did that happen? In a simple and smart way! The well-known advertising agency Telia & Pavla/BBDO ran a full page ad entitled "Sometimes goodbye means au revoir!"

The announcement/advertisement was saying "goodbye" to one of the company's longstanding and important clients, which was terminating its cooperation and moving to another – competing – agency! Unbelievable? Yes, but true! Now why would a company publicly say "goodbye" to a client that was going to work with a competitor? Was this a crazy or a clever move? Many of those seeing the advertisement asked themselves precisely that.

If we look more closely at the content of the full-page announcement/advertisement, we can say that the agency, having praised the close, trusting relationship and the excellent cooperation that it had enjoyed for the previous 10 years with its client, was actually saying "au revoir" (the French phrase might be translated as "until we meet again"). It was saying goodbye in front of the entire readership of Cyprus' top selling daily. But by saying "au revoir", it was saying a lot more too… It was leaving the door open for future cooperation with the client. It maintained its own value and quality by referring to its good relations with the client and the excellent service it had always provided. It behaved properly, above and beyond any interests, essentially putting the client in the position of wondering "What happens if this new deal doesn't work out?"

I shall never forget reading that full-page advertisement and seeing the agency's unprecedented gesture, one which provides significant benefits and lessons to all of us, for our professional and personal lives, such as:

! Expressing a positive culture and a value system since, in its announcement, the agency showed gratitude and appreciation above all.

! Investing in the future, leaving the door open for a client to return.

! Distinguishing the agency itself as one that recognises that patience and persistence pay off in the long term. A "no" from a client today may simply mean "not yet".

! Attracting the reader through the brief but substantial wording of the announcement.

I ended my study of the full-page advertisement by recalling one of the first lessons that I received from my mother, Miranda, at the start of my career. It was the saying, "Never burn your bridges of communication!".

For the first time, through that bold insertion in the newspaper, I understood how important it is not only not to burn our bridges of communication with our clients/customers but to appreciate, recognise and thank those who have offered us things and may offer us more in the future. Bridges exist in our lives to connect us with people. Keep them open!

V

CONTACTS

*"It's not what you know or who you know,
but who knows you!"*

Anonymous

I am sure that you have heard the well-known saying, *"It's not what you know but who you know"*. This was true during the Industrial Revolution. In today's Information Era, however, I am of the opinion that the saying has changed to *"It's not what you know or who you know, but who knows you!"*

The Internet and the way its use has spread have changed the 'rules of the game'. The Internet has brought wealth from one group of people to another, which may include the people of Amazon (www.amazon.com), one of the first big companies to embrace and understand its power, which started selling online. Thanks to the Internet, a new redistribution of wealth has taken place.

To use words that are often (and erroneously) attributed to Charles Darwin, "It is not the strongest of the species or the most intelligent that survives. It is the one that is the most adaptable to change." So it is today that in order to manage and to stand out, it would be a good idea to build your network, to take care of your own social networking. As the saying goes, *"Your network will determine your net worth"*.

The people with whom you spend most of your time influence your personality. Their experiences, ideas, education and personality affect your being. The average of all their positive and negative elements is reflected in you. In other words, you are the average of the people with whom you spend most of your time. The secret is to spend time with people who have goals, who wish to make progress and not take backward steps, people who are positive and not miserable and, finally, with people who are adaptable to the changes that the times impose on us. In our grandparents' day, people appreciated hard work; in today's world, people appreciate and are willing to pay well for ideas, hence the subtitle of this book: *24 Simple Ideas to Boost Your Business and Your Life.*

Ideas will come through the exchange of views with notable people and notable people will come through networks. Try to find the leaders in their field, those who are progressive and, in many cases, innovative. By being with the "right" people, you will start to think, speak and act differently from the crowd. To be among the "right" people is, in itself, to distinguish yourself…

By reading the articles in this section, you will be in a position to:

* Realise the enormous influence that those around you have on your personality.

* Know how to choose, using the right criteria, the people you want to have around you who will lead you to success.

* Learn to care about those who are close to you, always leaving a positive memory behind you.

* Expand your contacts by investing in technology and making the correct use of the Internet.

* Make the most of your investment in human resources as a weapon against any financial crisis.

20

The Cheetah and the Dog

San Diego Zoo has a reputation as one of the best zoos in the world, possibly the very best. I was fortunate to visit it with my wife Christine in December 2011. We learned that there are more than 800 different species of the animal kingdom there and, in particular, about the superb collection of 4,000 exotic animals. It is also one of the few zoos to be home to giant pandas. Covering an area of 100 acres, San Diego Zoo is an earthly animal paradise and a living source of knowledge for anyone interested in learning about – and getting up close and personal with – all kinds of animals.

We were impressed by much more than the animals: the trained zookeepers for their wealth of knowledge, the innovative educational programmes offered to visitors and the fact that the ultimate aim of the zoo is to create and provide the most comfortable natural environment for the animals there, fully satisfying all their physical and emotional needs so that where they live is no different from their natural habitat.

What impressed us most, however, and left us speechless, was Karoo, a nine-year-old cheetah that had Sven Olaf, a golden retriever of the same age, as its best friend. Karoo and Sven Olaf are the result of a third generation of successful pairings of cheetahs and dogs. As I discovered, it all began some years ago when a young cheetah, Arusha, was chosen to be part of the area where public education programmes take place. However, because cheetahs are evidently nervous creatures prone to sudden outbursts and would possibly be a danger to the trainers and the public, it was decided that Arusha would be placed in the same area as a dog of the same age named Anna. Within a week, the two animals had become inseparable friends, eating together, sleeping one beside the other and each licking the other's ears as a sign of friendship.

Those of us who had or have a dog know indisputably that dogs have a calming and relaxing effect on us. It was precisely this influence that the coexistence with Anna had on the explosive, always moving cheetah. Arusha was calmed and pacified by Anna. This fact led those in charge of the zoo to place young cheetahs in the same living space as slightly older dogs so that the dog would take the initiative in the relationship and, with its milder, more stable character, would help the cheetah not to "go crazy" with nervous outbursts. The programme was hugely successful and it continues to this day.

The question for you is this: with whom are you paired? Who has a positive effect on your professional and personal life, as the dog on the life of the cheetah? Is there such a person in your life or not? Think about it. Who are those who are around you every day and have been easily influenced by your moves and reactions? Which of your own activities are the result of the influence of those closest to you?

My experience has taught me that we are the average of the professional level of the 5 people with whom we associate. In other words, if you spend time with Maria (who has a professional level of 9 out of 10, Chryso (6 out of 10), Christis (8 out of 10), Savvas (10 out of 10) and Yianna (7 out of 10), you have a professional level of 8 out of 10 (because the average of your five friends' professional level is 8 (9+6+8+10+7=40÷5=8).

In their book *Body Language*, Allan and Barbara Pease correctly refer to studies that have shown that 50% of our gestures and habits are inborn, i.e. we are born with them (e.g. babies born blind or deaf laugh and cry without having seen or heard anyone do it) and 50% of our gestures and habits have been gained – we have learnt them from those around us (e.g. mother and daughter walk in the same way, football fans make the same gestures) For the 50% of our gestures and habits that we can determine and which will affect our personal and professional life, we "have a duty" to choose them carefully. We have an "obligation" to make a conscious choice of the people who are right for us to have them close to us and to have a bond with them. Because this choice will have repercussions on our life. And just as the dog has a positive influence on the cheetah's personality, so too will our choices ultimately be responsible for our professional progress and personal happiness. So find the people around you who are influencing you. Where are they leading you?

21

38 Years of Memory

Dick Jordan was no ordinary teacher. He was one of those few teachers who make a big difference. From 1962 and for four decades he taught hundreds of students at the George Washington High School in Denver, Colorado. From his first year at the school, he had an original idea: at the end of each school year he would issue an open invitation to all his students for a reunion on the steps of the Public Library on the first day of the new millennium, 1 January 2000.

On the "day of judgment" some 300 former students gathered on the steps of the library to honour their favourite teacher and to fulfil his wish. When journalists asked the students, now adults, how they had remembered to attend the meeting 30-40 years after receiving the invitation, they all answered unhesitatingly: *"Because Mr Jordan really cared for us! He taught us how to think and question, how to judge and not to just accept whatever we read in books. He taught us to question what was in the history books. His influence was such that he even inspired one of our classmates to become a teacher too."*

One of the three hundred people present at the reunion was the husband of one of Mr Jordan's former students. It had been his wife's wish shortly before she died of cancer that he should attend, given that she would not be alive on the predetermined date.

It was not by chance that Jordan managed to gather so many people for a meeting that he had organised 40 years previously. When he began his teaching career, his only possessions were his knowledge, his positive attitude and his concern for his students. Coming from a poor family, he wore the same suit for three years and, half-jokingly, he told the students to bring him a dollar on 1 January 2000 because he might need it by then. The former students remembered this detail too and each took $1 to the reunion. The sum of $300 was given to charity.

What was special about Dick Jordan? What was it that made him so loved back then and many years later too? Obviously, it was the fact that he cared about his students, all together and each one separately. He had what leadership guru John C. Maxwell considers an important characteristic of a leader: the ability to care for and look after all the people in his professional circle.

I firmly believe that what we take with us when we leave this life is what we leave behind... and what we leave behind us is nothing more or less than the lives of other people that we have touched and influenced positively. It is the mark and influence that we have on our children, the guidance we give them to become genuinely good people. For this reason, we can all model ourselves on Dick Jordan and be responsible for the positive memory we leave behind us so that our "students" remember a planned meeting with precision... even 38 years later!

22

A Window on the World

In the course of my cooperation with a very well-known offshore company to which I had been recruited to provide consultancy services, I found myself having to take an extremely difficult decision, together with the Management of the company. Two equally worthy graduates of the same university, holding the same degree and the same qualifications, were candidates for a single job vacancy.

It was a pleasant "headache" given that we had two apparently equal young graduates in line for a single managerial position. A position of crucial importance for the organisation's strategic interests, not only on the island but in the broader Middle East business sector. The annual salary would be around €55,000 plus additional financial benefits. All this, as you can easily realise, left no room for mistakes; indeed, it obliged us to take a difficult decision.

After a long brainstorming session and a great deal of thought, we came to our decision about which of the two candidates would be given the job. However, before we announced anything, I was given permission to check the profiles of both candidates on Facebook, LinkedIn and Twitter and to search Google for their names. The results left us speechless. The Facebook profile of the one we had chosen was littered with obscene language and gestures! Obscenities about political parties and beliefs that were not his own, about football teams he didn't support and much more. We were looking through an "open window" and we could see his world and very probably his character too. Naturally, we proceeded to hire the other candidate.

The rapid growth of technology and the arrival of the Internet in our lives (1991) have transformed the search for information into a simple game for every individual or professional. At this juncture let me make a simple and brief reference to the three social media that I personally use for my searches and for communicating with friends online, thereby building my own online profile. I am sure that you will find some of my suggestions and ideas useful.

1. **LinkedIn:** LinkedIn is one of the most powerful professional networking and search tools. It has tens of millions of members whose numbers are multiplying daily. Understanding the power of LinkedIn is extremely important for your personal and professional success. LinkedIn helps you build a virtual network of business

people on three levels: those who know you (1st level connections), those who know the people who know you (2nd level connections) and those who know the people who know the people who know you (3rd level connections). LinkedIn provides a mass of connections that you can use to your benefit. Through LinkedIn you can study the profile of a future customer before you meet him/her. You can also read endorsements of the individual in whom you are interested so as to see what close associates have to say about him/her. Through a search of the company you can find out who is in a specific position that affects your interests so as to better organise your contact with that person. It is not by chance that many services recruit or announce their recruitment through LinkedIn.

2. **Facebook:** For most people, Facebook is the star of today's social media. With more than 900 million users (2012), based on today's figures, if Facebook was a country it would have the 3rd largest population on the planet, behind China and India! My own experience has shown me that, since Facebook entered our lives, we no longer search to find out what's happening to our friends and acquaintances and even strangers as in the past; now the news comes and finds us. A typical example of catching up through Facebook is the fact that I only found out that my best friend had sprained his ankle when I saw his photo on Facebook! More than 300 million pieces of information including links, news, stories, vacancies, notes and photographs are uploaded and shared on Facebook every day. A classic example of Facebook use is the above story of the two candidates for a job. Personally, I would advise

every friend and associate of mine to be very careful about what they put on Facebook and how. Personal opinions on burning issues, political beliefs and rivalries should be off limits. Facebook, in most instances, gives you a clear picture of the interests, beliefs and business of your future client/customer and associate and even – who knows? – your future spouse!

3. **Twitter:** More than 500 million people have a Twitter account (2012) and tens of millions of tweets are posted every day. Today, Twitter is one of the best micro-blogging, social networking platforms as well as one of the best social marketing sites in the world. When you have a Twitter account you can send messages containing a maximum of 140 characters. These messages (professional or personal) can be read by anyone online. Companies can send messages (tweets) with a link to their website or to a product that is available, for example, as a special offer. I personally use Twitter as a search engine when writing my books. At any moment you can see real-time conversations and information related to the issue you are interested in. I also use Twitter to send out a daily message containing a saying of mine, e.g. *"If you want to get ahead, you have to think ahead"*.

As in real life, so it is in the world of social media that the quality of the relationship depends directly on the time you invest in it. Make sure that you are investing quality time and grey matter in your online relationships. Always bear in mind that anything you say online immediately belongs to everyone. If you slip, you may regain your balance but if your tongue or your writing slips, you cannot take them back.

So make proper use of these three examples of social media in such a way as to gain benefits for your personal life and your professional career. Make the Internet your greatest ally, not your worst enemy!

23

Billion-dollar Relationships

It was 22 July 2009 when I realised how important human relationships are. How did this come about? It was all because of an unusual news item on the Internet.

The well-known pioneer in online sales of books and much more, Amazon (www.amazon.com), had bought Zappos (www. zappos.com), a company whose name was unknown to most of us, for the extraordinary sum of $1.2 billion.

On hearing this, anyone would wonder what kind of huge company Zappos was and what innovative product or area it was dealing in to make Amazon invest such a huge amount in order to gain control of it. And yet, it was not like that at all. On the contrary! Zappos was a small company by American standards, employing 1,247 people when it was bought by Amazon in 2009 and it was in the business of…selling shoes. Yes, you read it correctly: selling shoes!

So what had attracted Amazon? What was it that made Zappos a unique and outstanding business opportunity? It was first and foremost the close, friendly ties it had developed with its customers. These fantastic ties were admired and probably envied not only by its competitors but by most American and global companies. Its greatest admirer, though, was Amazon which invested so much money in order to be part of this success.

How did Zappos manage to put itself in such a privileged position? Specific decisions and actions taken by the company led it to success:

* Initially, the company promised to "deliver wow through service" in every contact with its customers. There are countless examples of how Zappos employees have spent over 3-4 hours on the phone patiently and good-naturedly dealing with customer complaints until they were

satisfactorily resolved. It is not by chance that the company may have the most loyal and longstanding customers anywhere in the world.

Also, Zappos promised to take back any pair of shoes up to 365 days after the day of purchase without question and paying the postage for sending and returning the shoes! Note the example of the girl who, for four years, would buy a new pair of shoes every Monday and return it every Friday. And although Zappos knew that she was taking advantage of the company to wear new shoes every week, it never failed to supply them!

An important innovation was the creation of the Zappos Hero Academy with the aim of helping newly-recruited members of staff to adapt and adopt the Zappos culture. It is worth noting the example of Zappos CEO Tony Hsieh who offered $2,000 to anyone resigning on the first day after passing a 4-week training programme. Asked by a reporter why such a large amount was on offer, Hsieh said that this was the best way of maintaining the company's culture and values since the person who would take the money would never have had a career at Zappos. As he explained, "it's a small price to pay to maintain the high standard of customer service that we have already set".

Finally, Zappos has identified 10 core values which every member of the company is expected to embrace within a short time. On finishing the training programme, every Zappos employee is expected to be able to recite them at any time.

The above decisions and activities by Zappos are a rarity in the business world. This is why I am convinced that what drove Amazon to invest more than $1 billion in the company was all to do with the invaluable relations that Zappos had created with its huge customer base. The economy may be in trouble but not Zappos! And you, too, can protect yourself against any financial crisis by investing, not only on technology but mainly in your human resources, by developing friendly and sincere ties with your clients/customers and associates, based always on their best interests.

24

IN LIEU OF A POSTSCRIPT...

The Mirror

In Cyprus I see around five traffic accidents every month. That is the same number as the years I spent in the UK when I was a student, during which time I also witnessed five accidents. Five accidents a month in Cyprus, five accidents in five years in the UK! This is truly disproportionate. I once asked a British taxi driver about the tiny number of accidents: "What makes you such good drivers?" His reply, which admittedly gave me cause for concern, was short and to the point: "We hardly ever look in the mirror!"

Unfortunately, few people have this mentality in the course of their lives. There is nothing more damaging to your future prospects than spending the present while remaining stuck in and thinking about the past. The unfaithful spouse, the wrong professional move, your high blood sugar levels, the fall in your company's turnover during the past year and so many other thoughts about the past can poison your present and your future. Whatever has been done cannot be undone, whatever has been written cannot be unwritten; these are things that you cannot change; they belong to the past. Don't sit there feeling sorry for yourself and worrying about what has happened. See the past as a guide and a teacher for what you will do in the future. Don't let the past hold you back, fixated on yesterday.

You may be one of those people who, for some months now, have been running non-stop from one interview to another, from one company to the next, eager to hand over a CV in the hope of

finding a job. And you may have returned disappointed by the many negative replies and even by replies that were never given. You may be one of those salespeople who have received multiple negative responses from associates due to high prices. If you belong to either category or any other and you have experienced disappointment, don't give up, don't focus on past failures.

When you look into the mirror of your life, don't see only negative memories. Look ahead. You will see the best things that are to come through the windscreen of the vehicle of your life. With your every slip, with each "accident" as your guide, move on, all the wiser into the future. Always have your eyes firmly fixed on the road ahead and not in the mirror that leads you backwards because opportunities are always in front of you, never behind!

Have a good journey...

About the Author

Michael R. Virardi began his career without any particular financial problems, but he did not choose to simply take what the family business offered him. With an aspiration to do more, he founded his company MRV Simple Techniques Ltd[2] through which he provides solutions and advice to both individuals and organisations through training seminars, lectures and tutorials on a group or one-to-one basis, as well as his motivational speaking appearances.

MRV Simple Techniques has already shown impressive results, and is the outlet through which Michael realizes his goals to help the world of sales and business to improve and grow significantly.

Michael places great importance on continuous ongoing study and research, in order to maximize the impact of his abilities and to keep enriching his knowledge.

He describes himself as an eclectic reader as well as a collector and creator of information. He spends a great deal of time reading or listening to programmes, he attends countless seminars in Cyprus and abroad, taking care to keep constantly informed and updated in order to provide the best possible solutions to his clients.

Michael firmly believes that even the average person has abilities that, with the correct management and development, can bring personal and even financial gains. In his capacity as a motivational speaker, Michael has also created a series of popular DVDs and CDs in Greek and English, focusing on issues such as Differentiation, Leadership, Teamwork, Setting Goals, Time Management, Customer Service and Sales Solutions.

---

[2] By visiting his personal website at www.michaelvirardi.com you can find out more about Michael and the work he does through seminars, lectures and addresses.

He is also a registered trainer with the Human Resource Development Authority of Cyprus, an active member of the Advisory Board of the University of Nicosia and a Visiting Lecturer at the same university.

He has given countless seminars and been a speaker at company symposia held by several prestigious organisations, including among others:

Cyprus Shipping Chamber	*Aker Solutions*
Alpha Mega	*Eureka*
Marks & Spencer	*Interlaw*
University of Cyprus	*Hellenic Bank*

In Michael is also available for motivational speaking opportunities, and can deliver inspirational messages for both corporate and other private events, with a focus on inspiring audiences to seek personal development and differentiation to succeed.

In 2013, Michael was invited to give a speech to the students of the Swiss Education Group at the largest annual hospitality event in Montreux, Switzerland.

In 2013, Michael also gave a lecture at University College London (UCL) in the UK - voted as the 4th best University in the world in 2013 - to the students and the faculty.

Michael has also spoken in 2013 (Nicosia, Cyprus) and 2014 (Ankara, Turkey) at the prestigious TEDx talks.

Michael R. Virardi is a shareholder and co-owner of Virardi[3] , the best-known professional catering equipment firm in Cyprus.

In Michael's own words, his vision is "to use my enthusiasm and knowledge to provide inspiration and support to people so that they may become happy and active, and to show them how to stand out from everyone else around them. My ultimate aim is to help them reach their goals".

---

[3] **www.virardi.com**

If you have enjoyed this book, don't miss...

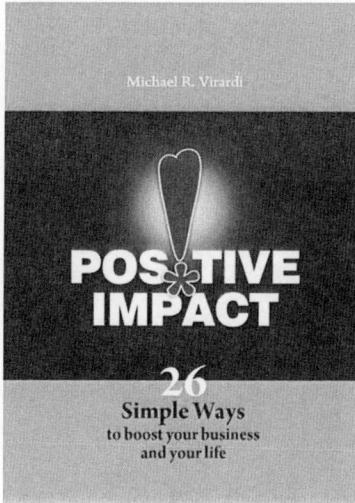

How could advice on professional and personal development be inspired by a delayed flight, a scent, a tenor or even... an apple core?

Sounds unlikely? Perhaps, but everything happening around us can be turned into useful and valuable knowledge.

Available on www.amazon.con and on www.PositiveImpactBook.com fincluding versions for iPad, Kindle and more.

! Notes